Choices! Choices! Choices!

Responsibility: *Making and Living With Choices*

Authors
Betty Gouge, Ph.D.
J. Thomas Morse, M.A.
John Eickmeyer

Research and Editing
Lyn Huntley, Ph.D.
Mary Thrash, M.A.
Teri Gathings, M.S.
Linda Stanislao, B.S.

Illustrations
Linda Bleck
Cathie Bleck
(character development)

Published by Family Skills, Inc., Dallas, Texas.
Distributed to the Book Trade by
Kampmann & Company, Inc., New York, New York.

*Family Skills, Inc. wishes to acknowledge and express our sincere thanks
to the hundreds of children and parents who contributed to the research,
design, development and testing of KidSkills™ interpersonal skills series.*

Hello! My name's Heada.
I'm little, it's true.
But I make big choices,
And you can choose, too!

I choose toys I like,
And the games I will play.
I think I will be a
Jet pilot today!

I choose to pretend
That I'm flying so high.
My bed is the plane
That I ride through the sky.

In the tub I can choose
To have bubbles or not.
I choose that the water
Is just right — not too hot.

I pick what to play with —
My ship or my boat,
My turtle or fish,
Or my duck that can float.

I choose things to draw.
I draw every day.
I draw what I want
In my own special way.

I choose to draw pictures
Of horses and dogs,
And spacemen and Eskimos,
Princes and frogs.

Most mornings I choose
How to do my own hair.
I look in the mirror
And see myself there.

Mom helps me make pigtails
Or one nice, long braid.
Do you like the ponytail
We have just made?

I pick out my clothes
And my mom lets me choose —
My red shorts or blue jeans?
Pink sneakers? Brown shoes?

And sometimes Mom lets me
Put wild things together —
Stripes! Polka Dots!
And a hat with a feather!

At breakfast I choose
The fruit juice I'll drink.
Grapefruit or orange,
What do *you* think?

Would you choose grapefruit
Or orange — which one?
Sometimes choosing's hard,
And sometimes it's fun.

Outside I can choose
To play many fun things.
I might ride my trike
Or go play on the swings.

I'll dig in the sandbox
Or climb up a tree.
Whatever I play
Is decided by me!

Before my friends come over,
I choose toys to share.
My most special toys,
I put away with great care.

Then my friends come to visit,
And what we have to do
Is choose who plays with which toy.
We have lots of fun, too.

When I chose the paints,
My friend chose the clay.
Then I wanted to trade,
But he said, "No way!"

"Now, Heada," said Mom,
"You must wait till he's through.
You made your own choice,
So the paints are for you."

I chose a banana,
Took two bites and said,
"I'd rather have cherries.
May I have them instead?"

"Now, Heada," said Mom,
"You have chosen your treat.
You cannot change now.
You chose what to eat."

When I wanted a treat
And my mom said, "Not now."
I cried and I screamed.
She said, "No!" anyhow.

Mom said, "You may choose
To cry loudly, my dear.
But go into your room,
For I don't want to hear."

I cried in my room
As I stomped on the floor.
And when I felt better,
I opened the door.

"I don't want to cry
Anymore, Mom!" I said.
She gave me a hug
And said, "Let's talk, instead."

Sometimes there's *no* choice,
Like at nap time each day.
I don't want to rest!
I would much rather play!

I can choose not to like it.
I can choose to frown
And make a mad face!
Yet I still must lie down!

I can choose my own thoughts
As I lie on my bed.
I wonder how zebras
Would look green and red.

I think about flying
Clear up to the moon —
Or making a friend
With a funny baboon.

Once I chose to go out
With no hat on my head.
The cold wind blew hard.
My mom saw me and said,

"If you choose to stay out,
Then you must wear a hat,
Or a hood, and a scarf.
There's no choice about that."

And there's no choice about
Chores that have to be done,
Such as picking up toys,
But I *can* make it fun.

Yes, I *can* choose to make it
A game I can play.
I pretend it's a race.
Hurry! Put things away!

Sometimes I make choices
When we go to the store.
Mom says I can buy
One toy and no more.

Oh, too many choices!
I don't know what to do.
Mom helps me by saying,
"Choose one of these two."

Mom makes sure I have
Some good choices to make,
Such as spinach or carrots,
Which one shall I take?

And do I want roast beef
Or chicken that's fried?
Which one would *you* choose?
Go ahead! You decide!

I choose shows I like
When I'm watching TV.
Mom says I can watch
Channels 1, 2, or 3.

I love seeing puppets
And clowns and cartoons.
I can watch for one hour
Weekday afternoons.

I choose thoughts and feelings.
I choose things to do.
I choose toys and pictures
And foods I like, too.

I choose clothes to wear
From my hat to my shoes.
I feel very proud
That I'm able to choose.

When you make *your* choices,
You'll feel so proud, too!
It's all part of being
That wonderful YOU!

Other books from Family Skills:

Preschool:

Self-Esteem: *Adjusting to New Experiences*
Feelings: *Experiencing Feelings*
Responsibility: *Understanding and Accepting Limits*
Self-Awareness: *Accepting and Knowing Myself*
Friendship: *Sharing and Taking Turns*

School Age:

Self-Esteem: *Being a Friend to Myself*
Cooperation: *Working Together*
Feelings: *Dealing With Feelings*
Listening: *Giving and Getting Attention*
Friendship: *Keeping Friends*
Friendship: *Making Friends*
Responsibility: *Making and Carrying Out a Plan*
Self-Talk: *Thinking and Feeling Good When Things Go Wrong*